30 Days of Inspiration

By
Jennie Martin

ISBN: 978-0692502983

TABLE OF CONTENTS

1. The Piano

As I trudged towards my next appointment I heard the faint noise of music. I smiled, knowing the sound was coming from just around the corner. The Mayo Clinic had placed a small upright piano on the edge of a major basement walkway between buildings and elevators..

Oftentimes the piano sat quietly, undisturbed as the bustle of patients from all over the world sought their miracle at the medical mecca. But sometimes in the afternoon a volunteer would venture to make the keys come alive. People stopped and listened if time allowed, drinking in the tunes that rang of encouragement and comfort.

As I grew closer, I realized there was a bigger crowd than usual. When I turned and peered through, I soon saw why. As "The Tennessee Waltz" played slower than its typical beat, a small group of women sang along, slightly off key. But no one cared, for all eyes were on the couple dancing to the music.

The silver-haired gentleman led his bride across the floor as if at a glorious ball. He twirled his love and did his version of the waltz, smiling as if he were a million miles away and yet present with the woman of his dreams in this moment.

As she gazed tenderly towards him, there was no one else in the room, or in their lives. They were not at the Mayo Clinic. She was not wearing a clumsy, ill-fitting wig that tilted as he pulled and pushed her to the music. Their time together was not limited by the ravages of disease; there was no grim prognosis; she was not dying.

As the music ended the man knelt down to be at eye level with the woman. He held her hands and gingerly turned her face towards his. The room was hushed as the knight caressingly kissed his princess. For a moment, time stood still. He loved her to the fullest, seeing so much more than the frail woman who scarcely filled her chair.

When it was over, sustained applause greeted the couple, which seemed the first time they noticed their audience. After it subsided, he stepped behind her and firmly gripped the handles of her wheelchair as they disappeared into the crowd. It was time for their next appointment. The piano had provided its therapy.

2. Salt

I smelled it as soon as I walked into the room, as the unmistakable scent of lilac infused the air. I couldn't help but notice it came from Jonna's desk. There she was, extracting lotion out of its bottle with a giant syringe, only to transfer it to a smaller container. I never did understand the logic of her efforts.

Jonna was a simple soul who worked as a Medical Assistant in the inner city medical clinic where I served as the medical social worker. With space at a premium, my desk was crammed into the same room where the nurses wrote their reports.

Though Jonna and I came from very different backgrounds, we had in common a faith in the Lord and a mutual respect for each other. I noticed that she often pulled an oversized King

James Bible from her desk during work breaks so she could complete her daily reading.

I learned that Jonna took the scriptures literally but I never realized the extent of her unique grasp of the Word until one particularly hot summer day. It was over 100 degrees and not only would the building's air conditioner not budge, but the water was off, too.

The administration decided to stay open as patients kept pouring into our facility. Jonna was so busy assisting her doctor that she was going to miss her break. As she saw me walk by, scrounging fans to take to another waiting room full of sweltering pregnant women, she pulled me aside.

"Jennie," she pleaded, "please go to the vending machine and get me some Fritos. I got to have some."

"Jonna, it's so hot and there are no cold drinks left; you're going to get really thirsty if you eat something so salty."

She looked at me in desperation. When our eyes met I could tell this was no ordinary request for a snack. "Don't you remember the

Bible says we're the salt of the earth?" Referring to Matthew 5:13, she continued. "If we lose our salt, we'll be tossed out. I can't lose my salt, Jennie. I can't lose my salt."

There it was, a faith so earnest and yet so simple that Jonna would do anything to get salt because she believed that it would please her Savior. There was nothing left to do but dig through my purse for enough money to purchase a bag of salty corn chips.

It never occurred to me to ridicule my sister in Christ or to convince her that Jesus was using salt as an illustration. She was determined to act out her beliefs the way she understood them, even if it meant thirst and discomfort for her. As I reflect back on that scorching day, I smile as I realize I can learn a lot about dedicated obedience from Jonna. Maybe we all can.

3. Faithful

"Don't stay out too late!" we laughingly teased. It was great fun watching Paul and Marge hold hands as they traipsed down the porch steps and out to the car for another date. My mother-in-law was school-girl happy, joyfully falling in love after being widowed for so many years.

What was even more amazing was how Paul entered our lives. He and his wife had both been only children. Since his parents were already gone, Paul moved from Texas to Missouri when his wife died after a long battle with cancer. He resolved to take care of his in-laws there.

Paul had fulfilled his vow to "love, honor and cherish till death do us part". Now here he was, taking his vows to the next level, caring for her parents in faithfulness to His Father.

Paul and Marge were both rewarded for Paul's unselfishness. They met at church, soon began sitting on the same row and then attending the same functions. It was not long before they became known as a couple. They pledged their lives to each other on a summer day in July at a small country church.

God blessed them with almost two years of marriage before Paul succumbed to cancer. In His infinite wisdom, the Lord knew Paul would need a help-mate as he traveled through the valley of the shadow of death. Marge was that woman, lovingly serving until he was called home.

Now it is my parents who are in need. I cherish the way my husband cheerfully comes alongside to help my siblings and me in any way he can. He is my devoted life partner, obedient to the call made by our Redeemer to be upright and dependable in all things.

I thank God for those who prove faithful in their walk with God, manifested in how they serve those unable to give them anything in return.

4. No Rags in the Kingdom

I was excited when asked to serve as Mission Director for Vacation Bible School (VBS) at the small church where we worshipped at the time. With the job came the opportunity to choose a mission to which the children would donate during the week. Determined to try something different, I selected a local homeless shelter with which our church was affiliated. It would be the benefactor of all the gifts the children would bring.

During the week of VBS the elementary-aged kids learned that this shelter was for families: moms and dads and children who did not have a home. They needed food and clothing and all the very basics of life. More than anything, however, these families yearned for someone to genuinely care about them; and they needed the hope of Christ.

While the VBS attendees proudly brought their nickels and dimes, our collection expanded beyond money. They were encouraged to bring canned food and toiletries, as well as gently used clothing and toys. And bring they did! The gifts kept pouring in, presenting a challenge as to how I was going to get them all delivered. God is good and these children are amazing, I told myself.

Then I began to look through the mountains of bags and boxes of donations. Of course there was a substantial amount of useable food and other items. But what greatly disturbed me was what else I found. There is no other way of describing it – some people had given bags of things that should have been tossed in a garbage dump.

I saw mounds of soiled clothes, broken toys, games with missing pieces and inappropriate books and magazines. Simply put, it was their trash. Now it was sitting at the church, with the intended recipients being families at a homeless shelter who had virtually nothing to their names. I was mortified.

The parents of the children who literally sent junk to VBS to be presented as a missions offering were teaching their children that these poor families were not worthy of our best; worse, they were being taught that God is not worthy of our best. I felt a great sorrow for them.

Whenever we prepare to give, may it done cheerfully and with the knowledge that it is our finest, given in love. When we give, we are called to give as unto the Lord. May we not be guilty of donating rags to the kingdom.

5. Friday

As His body trembled under the weight of the wood, He scanned the crowd of onlookers, His gaze meeting the eyes of teary loved ones. Despite the agony of His wounds, He sought to reassure the followers brave enough to accompany Him on this tortuous journey - the one He beseeched His Father to avoid if there be any other way.

He struggled up the hill, no longer able to carry the crudely made cross. There He submitted to the hammering; the torn flesh; the pain of human suffering which marked the sacrifice He came to make. He allowed no sedative, no relief of the throbbing torment; He would endure the full measure of the sentence.

As He hung there, momentarily suspended in eternity, the fullness of the cost for the salvation of all who would believe was paid. His God-eyes saw the faithful generations past who had believed that God would provide a Redeemer. Suspended above the timeline of all humanity, He then glimpsed into the future, seeing the generations on this side of the cross that would put their trust in Him.

He saw you; He saw me. He knew our sin, yet He still chose to die to deliver us. Thank God for that Friday.

6. Worth the Wait

With a head full of lice and an attitude of threatening swagger, it was no surprise that 14-year-old Cindy had no friends. She was eight months pregnant that late November day when she grudgingly slumped into the counseling room and fell into a chair, refusing to speak. She didn't care that her head was crawling with tiny insects; at least that prevented people from getting too close. She had literally perfected keeping outsiders at bay.

Cindy had long since grown numb to the world around her. Her defense mechanisms were fully operational as she silently dared me to make her communicate. I knew I had to somehow join her in the quiet of her layered hurt. How could I expect her to talk if I didn't respect the earnestness of her well-built fortress? There were few words spoken that hour. They consisted of me telling her she was worth waiting for and later asking if she liked to color. The slightest nod ignited my prayers. I spent the time imploring the heavenly Father to release her from the scars of her past.

The next time I laid crayons and coloring sheets on the table, fanning them just enough to show an adorable dog smiling at a child. I was prepared to wait again. Once again I initially met stiff resistance – and then it happened. At the end of the session Cindy grabbed the sheet of the dog and stormed off with it. Somehow memories were stirred of a dog who loved her when no one else did. This was the gateway she used to start working in therapy.

Before long, Cindy no longer needed lice and a bad attitude for safety barriers. She asked me to help her make an adoption plan for her baby girl. She had one stipulation that was non-negotiable. The adoptive family had to have an older brother to protect his little sister, something she desperately wished she could have had.

I imagine God must have smiled when we got the call that a family had been located. They had adopted a now 5-year-old boy and had been praying for God to bless them with a girl. Amy was born the week before Christmas and Cindy summoned the courage to place her into the arms of her new parents.

We cannot erase the pain others have caused. But we are called to love the unlovely, no matter what that looks like. It is always worth the wait. After all, that is what God does for each of us.

7. Nail Polish and a Nightgown

These days having your head shaved can be considered a status symbol. For me, it represented just one more humiliation. I was sick again and missing a younger sister's college graduation. While outside breathed the promise of spring, I was trapped inside the prison of my hospital room. At twenty-three I felt like leftovers in the back of the refrigerator – old; stale; forgotten by a world that was passing me by.

I had a severe case of meningitis and the I.V. medication had become too diluted to be effective, meaning more drastic action was necessary. A petite funnel called an Omaiah Reservoir was placed at the base of my brain and spinal cord. The idea was that medicine would be injected straight into the spine, giving me a better chance to recover.

There I was, with a huge chunk of hair missing from the right side of my head, shaved to allow access to insert the device. All I saw when I looked in the mirror was a muddled mess, too weak to hold up a hair dryer long enough to dry my own hair.

I guess that's why what my oldest sister, Ruth, did the day of the graduation meant so much. She knew I felt isolated and alone, so she sent word she'd be arriving long before the rest of the family with a mysterious surprise. At last I had something to look forward to, to anticipate.

When Ruth arrived, she rummaged through my small shelf of belongings, long since neglected since I was unable to use anything it contained. She then approached my bed with a stack of beautiful nightgowns. Their colors of spring contrasted markedly with the gray walls. Ruth waited patiently while I picked one. Then she gently unsnapped the dismal hospital-issue garb and helped me into the first "real clothes" I had worn in ages.

Then came the crowning moment: after rummaging in her bag, Ruth pulled out a bottle of nail polish. A real nightgown was one thing;

but this felt like extravagance beyond compare! She gingerly painted each nail to perfection, as if I were a princess preparing for a ball.

The surprise continued when she asked, "How would you like me to do something with your hair?" With great care she heated her curling iron and helped position me in the bed where she could reach my head. As she slowly brushed and curled what was left of my shorn crop, Ruth studiously avoided the bald spot that was accented by a cartoon bandage the nurses insisted on using.

Neither the nightgown, nor the nail polish, nor the innovative hairstyle changed the reality of my condition. But they accomplished a feat that was magical all on its own. They made me feel like a woman again. They provided the ray of hope I so desperately needed. I remembered that I was loved; I mattered. I will never forget the day my oldest sister used a small bottle of nail polish, a nightgown and a curling iron to transform my gloomy dungeon into a beauty spa.

8. Close Your Eyes

How I came to be in Duoc's hospital room as he lay dying was one thing. Getting the honor of comforting the man in English when his pain-ravaged mind longed for his native Vietnamese tongue was downright mystifying. A refugee from his war-ravaged country, he had no family in the states. As his health progressively worsened, he came less often to the community center where I worked. Then I heard he had been hospitalized.

I didn't know him well but realized his prognosis was not good. Laboring to breathe, Duoc was propped up in a chair by his bed when I entered. Thankfully, he recognized me. Suddenly we weren't two individuals in a patient/social worker relationship, a cultural lifetime apart. We were merely two children of the King, one sent to strengthen the other.

There was no pretense. He told me right away he knew he was dying.

Duoc had experienced such a depth of loneliness in life, having been literally cast out of his home as a baby because his mother was unmarried. Now here he was by himself in a foreign land. What he dreaded most was the idea of dying alone. He was a new Christian with no idea of what heaven might be was like or what to expect. In the haze of his pain he wondered if he was truly loved.

Forgetting that I was unfamiliar with his language, Duoc whispered that there was a Bible under his pillow. He couldn't focus his eyes; would I read it to him? His Bible was filled with strange hieroglyphics that registered no meaning for me, yet he did not want me to take the time to locate an English translation. Instead, Duoc sat across from me in the dimly lit room as I spoke of the joy there would be when he entered heaven. I told him of a place where there would be no more loneliness, or fear, or tears of sorrow.

After a while, I noticed his breathing had changed. Assuming he had fallen asleep, I stopped talking. After a moment his eyes opened expectantly. "I'm still awake. I just want to keep my eyes closed; you keep telling me about heaven." And so I did.

I don't remember what all I said that day. I do know that we sat for a long time that afternoon, facing each other in chairs a few feet apart. One of us was set to return home to family; the other was near the threshold of heaven's gates - and he just wanted someone to accompany him part of the way. He did it with his heart open and his eyes closed.

(This is Part I of Duoc's story. For Part II, read "The Box.")

9. The Box

(This is Part II of Duoc's story. For Part I, read "Close Your Eyes".)

Duoc died a few short days after I visited him in the hospital. The community center's Vietnamese interpreter felt strongly that his body belonged to his mother and should be returned to his homeland. That's where I entered the picture. The interpreter would plan the memorial service; I was to take care of the returning.

Duoc was the first person I ever knew who was cremated so my learning curve was tremendous. I didn't have the slightest idea of the regulations on how to mail such a package to another country. Research indicated that not every nation accepted such a shipment. Thankfully, Viet Nam did. I studied the rules about how the ashes were to be sealed and the details regarding the labels for the outside of the box.

The box that was delivered to my desk disturbed me greatly, not because it held his cremated remains, but because that's all that was in it. I thought of how his mother would feel when she received it. She had not seen her son in years and now she was going to get a cardboard container, inside of which was a bag holding all that was left of him. My heart was heavy.

I was told that Duoc's mom did not know any English. Still, I felt compelled to write a letter, hoping someone could read it to her. I shared how his smile was so warm and friendly; that he worked hard and was greatly admired. I then assured her that he was now in heaven, no longer sick or in pain. I folded it solemnly and placed it on top of the bag of remains in the box. It should be the first thing she sees when the box is open, I reasoned - before she has to view her son's ashes.

I wondered what his mom's reaction would be to receiving the package. I hoped the letter would be at least a small comfort at such a sorrowful time. The memory of the box stays with me. It reminds me how fragile life is - and how glad I am that Duoc was already in heaven when it was mailed, worshipping at the throne.

10. He Sees

Mary stood there, huddled with the other women. Her friends were sobbing but no tears came for her. She had already wept a thousand teardrops in the nights leading up to this one. Now there was only numbness, and nothing left to do but wait for the agonizing vigil to end.

Her friends desperately wished to shield her from the sorrow; but that was impossible, for they felt it, too. They also realized that she had another more practical reason to worry. Soon Mary would be alone in the world with no way to support herself, an agonizing side effect to the anguish played out before them.

The women hugged, then held hands in solidarity, lingering together unobtrusively in the shadows. A few men scoffed at them but mostly they were ignored, nameless faces in the crowd of onlookers.

Mary didn't want to look, yet her eyes were drawn to the scene only a few yards away – her Son hanging limp on a cross; bloodied, bruised, exposed. When she did glance up, she saw the tender eyes of her Son gaze calmly into hers.

He broke the silence, speaking directly to her as He gasped for each precious breath. "'Dear woman, here is your son.'" With a simple turn of the head He then turned his attention to her nephew, John, one of the twelve. "'Here is your mother,'" he directed John.

Both Mary and John knew the intent of the Master's words. In Jesus' earthly absence John would have the responsibility of caring and providing for her. When Mary's eyes met his again, she couldn't help but smile faintly in gratitude, shaking her head in wonder.

With the weight of mankind's past, present and future sin upon Him, Jesus took the time and effort to think of His earthly mother and make arrangements for her future. He could so easily have tended solely to the monumental task set before Him, the redemption of creation. Yet in the midst of His agony He noticed one life, one need – and He met it.

What a blessing to know that as God keeps the earth spinning on its axis and tends to the mass of humanity, He sees us, individually. He sees; He loves; and He meets our needs – at the foot of the cross.

11. Sides

The sides of God are so diverse because He is so intensely real. Those who slander our faith contend that it is merely our imagination, an opiate or an escape from reality. But God appears that way only to those who haven't searched for His vast greatness, or wanted to see even a glimpse of Him. He is ready and willing to show Himself to anyone who truly desires to find Him.

When I become too content in my current perception of God, the Holy Spirit gently chides me to look a little further, to dig a little deeper, and to search a little more - to grasp more of Him. That is one of the key reasons why spending time with other Christians, drawing from their strength and support, is so vital. This is especially true in hard times. Every Christian, based upon her perceptions, has a bit, a piece, an insight, that I can learn from in my meager attempts to see more of God.

My dominant view of God is of a Father. He is Someone Who smiles and holds me to His breast, and still offers to carry me even when I rail against Him or grow angry at things I can't understand. My God views me in my weakness as a small child He cherishes and cares for despite the fact that I am not always so lovable. He is a God that will cause me to endure.

I have described my side of God partially to give Him thanks for all He has done for me, and partially to encourage each of you to show me your side. I need to know the sides of God others see to which I am now blind. We all need to share with each other. Only then can we gain a more complete understanding of the great omnipotence of our God.

(Excerpted from *Another at the Pool: When Healing Doesn't Come*)

12. Choco-Nut Noodle Logs

It was a dark and stormy night. That's how I typically start the story of the fateful night I created a dessert so peculiar that I have never made it since. It was time for a staff/resident party at work, my first at the Habilitation Center where I had been recently hired.

I didn't have much on hand and it really was storming. That's how I rationalized mixing the few ingredients I had on hand: lasagna noodles, chocolate chips and peanut butter. Who doesn't love chocolate and peanut butter together? An entire brand of candy is made on that premise. I merely needed a vessel for my merger.

I cooked the noodles and cautiously lifted them onto a cookie sheet so they wouldn't tear. I needed the curly sides as a decorative touch. With a touch of inspiration, I sliced the noodles, generously spreading peanut butter and microwave-melted chocolate on each piece before rolling them.

Hmmm. They looked starkly plain on top; they screamed for color. After a quick search I located a near empty bottle of chocolate syrup, which I excitedly drizzled on top of each carefully crafted morsel. I stood back and marveled at my creation. Who wouldn't love my genius?

But they needed a name. After all, what would I say when people asked what they were? After a moment I proudly decided an appropriate designation would be Choco-Nut Noodle Logs. They were chocolaty-peanut butter wrapped up in a noodle that one could call a log; enough said.

Well, people did ask. And one mentally challenged resident ran in fear after touching a piece. I had overlooked a significant factor – the cold noodle. It may look good but it wasn't well received. In the end, it did accomplish one embarrassing thing. My boss told me I didn't need to bring anything to future employee potlucks. What a way to start!

13. Light Switches and Noses

The sudden thud was followed instantly by loud wailing. The door burst open to reveal Eddy sobbing loudly and holding his nose in his hands. "What in the world happened?" I asked as I rushed to tend to him.

It was Sunday morning at church and I was herding a horde of children to the restroom. I was waiting in the hall for the kids to regroup, never quite knowing if the boys would behave given the temptation that sinks of water provided in unsupervised moments.

"Somebody turned the lights off and I ran into the wall," Eddy wailed. I quickly assessed the situation and noticed that Eddy was not bleeding. But since he was not going to be satisfied without medical attention, I was relieved when a make-shift ice pack produced a remarkably swift recovery.

Then it was time to locate the culprit. I calmly but firmly lined all the boys up against the wall and asked who had done it. I could not have been more surprised when my most well-behaved boy raised his hand, almost proudly. "I did," he announced.

I somehow retained the presence of mind to inquire, "Why did you turn the lights off?" His answer was matter-of-fact. "Because the sign says, "Please turn off the lights." That was it. The sign didn't say anything about being the last one out before actually darkening the place. He thought he was being obedient. He harbored no malice or ill will. He could read the posted sign and he was proud. How could I be mad?

As I reflect on all the times I act with good motives, yet without sufficient knowledge of the situation, I imagine I must exasperate God quite often. I only hope He still smiles – because He knows my heart.

14. Bear Hunt

I never associated innocent childhood play with an emergency room visit; I had no idea it could be that dangerous. Yet somehow I wound up in the hospital desperately trying to figure out what went wrong.

It all started when I enthusiastically agreed to lead a group of 3 and 4-year-olds for a week of Bible learning fun we call Vacation Bible School. So what if I didn't have much experience with that age group; what could go wrong?

One of the first things I discovered was that clocks don't seem to matter to little people. Every item on the night's agenda was completed so rapidly that there was a huge chunk of time to fill. I realized I had to think quickly before I had a mutiny of small humans vying for my attention.

I decided to engage the kids in a harmless bear hunt. It involved sitting (which was wonderful!) and the pitter-patter of hands on thighs as we traveled through woods and over mountains to hunt bears – only to finally discover a grizzly in a dark cave – and dash home, the sounds of our journey echoed in the thunderous clap of hands on our upper legs as we rushed towards safety.

Suffice it to say the hunt was an enormous success. The kids loved it and joyously insisted we keep hunting for the rest of our time together that fateful evening.

The next day I discovered the horror of badly bruised upper legs, indicative of numerous broken blood vessels. It looked appalling and I initially assumed it was related to my chronic illness. My husband, Mike, took me to the emergency room without hesitation. This appeared very serious.

It became evident right away that the nurses wanted nothing to do with Mike. One by one they pulled me away from him so they could talk to me alone. They were certain I had been beaten and that I would only feel comfortable confiding in them if they separated us.

Finally a doctor inquired more deeply into my recent activity. That's when it hit me; I was the victim of a self-inflicted bear hunt. Yes, I had broken my own blood vessels, something more easily accomplished in a body suffering from lupus and the necessary medications to combat its effects.

I typically work with older kids now. And if I am ever in a room with a group of little children expecting to be entertained, you better believe that anything we do won't involve hunting.

15. Edge of Eternity

The memory of his picture flashing across the screen will haunt me forever. August 7, 1998 was the day terrorism became personal for me. Reporters interrupted programming for breaking news: two U.S. embassies had been bombed.

How many were dead? Who was responsible? I paced the floor, pondering the larger implications of what was occurring. What I learned made a profound impact on my life, and it had nothing to do with geo-political divisions. The jolt hit me like a tidal wave when victims' pictures were shown and I recognized one of them. Among the dead in Kenya was a young service man from my home town. His name was Kevin.

What really bothered me was that I couldn't remember many details about his life. I had led our small church youth group when Kevin was in high school. He had drifted in and out and I had not taken any real time to follow up with him. I rationalized it at the time because I was busy with work and graduate school.

It seemed okay not to know that Kevin had married, had a two-year-old daughter and was stationed with military intelligence in Africa. People lose touch as life goes on. But I had neglected Kevin on the peripheral edges of eternity. I was responsible for his youth group at a crucial time in his life. How could I not take the time to reach out?

I don't know where Kevin stood with the Lord and I was not solely accountable for his eternal fate. But in the wake of the bombings, my heart stood still as I realized that eternity had beckoned someone whose life I had a real opportunity to impact – and I had ignored it.

Jesus told us that the fields are white and ready to be harvested. While I rationalized that my career choice itself was a gesture of obedience, God had already entrusted to me temporary care of part of His harvest. I overlooked it because I was waiting to be sent to another part of the field.

The reality finally hit that there are people all around me who are not ready for eternity to beckon. How many times have we been blinded to the truth of hungry souls right in our midst? They are on our streets, in our schools, at work; and even in our churches. Let us commit ourselves to not miss any more Kevins, who are even now on the edge of eternity.

16. Because Verlin Lives

Verlin lived for afternoon rides in the tram when he could feel the gentle breeze and bask in the sunlight on a warm day. At least that's what I initially thought. The first time I rode with him I noticed how quiet and focused he was. But instead of gazing at the birds overhead or the beauty of the trees, Verlin was intently concentrating on the ground. I soon found out why.

Before I realized what was happening Verlin jumped off and pounced on something. He lobbed it into his mouth, swallowing without blinking. It was a cigarette butt. Verlin didn't care a whit about the sun or the wind or the birds. He wanted the tram ride to get his fix of butts. That was it.

Unfortunately, Verlin's penchant for taste bud satisfaction went way beyond my imagination.

The man ate human waste. There's no polite way of putting it. His two favorite things to eat in the world were feces and cigarette butts.

The great irony was that Verlin was deathly afraid of liver. On the rare occasions when the evening meal included an entree of that detested meat, Verlin literally ran from it, screaming. The man had his principles.

I met him while working on a ward of severely mentally retarded individuals. These people could not hold conversations, or tell you when they were scared and wanted a hug. They were unable to verbally express their hopes and dreams, much less what they wanted to do that day. In this age when we publicly debate the merits of cost of care versus quality of life, I can't help thinking of all the Verlins in the world, the men and women who will never be able to care for themselves or live outside the walls of an institution. What do we owe them?

I don't know why Verlin's mind doesn't work the same way mine does. But I do know that he is alive, and that life matters. If we neglect to protect the mentally challenged, what other lives may someday be considered worth less or too expensive to assuage the convenience of the masses? We love because they live. It's that simple.

17. Unparalyzed

When Marge was first diagnosed with a brain tumor, no one knew exactly what to expect. After all, we didn't know what part of the brain would be affected. Radiation and chemotherapy staved off much of the damage for a time; but when it returned my mother-in-law became unable to move an entire side of her body.

Her queen sized bed was disassembled the day hospice arrived at her house, replaced by a modest hospital bed. The room would have looked barren if not for the family crowded close to her, whispering encouragement. What was thought to be a short vigil due to the advanced, aggressive return of the cancer became a months-long ordeal. We watched helplessly as the selfish disease lay claim to more of her functionality, grateful all the while that her thought processes were largely unaffected.

Why is God letting her suffer like this?" I was asked by a concerned friend. "Why doesn't He just take her home?" Marge had lived out a life of faithful obedience to her Christianity. Everyone around her knew that she was unafraid of death and ready to meet her Savior face to face. Why the agony?

I didn't have all the answers but I did know one thing. As I observed Marge on her death-bed I saw something amazing. She spent many of her waking moments pleading with the Holy Spirit on behalf of the people God had placed in her life. She didn't spend her days begging for more time. She was nearing the end of a life well lived and realized the importance of intercessory prayer.

Marge may have been unable to get out of bed or eat on her own. But when I remember her restless body waiting for the redemption of heaven, my goal is to live more like she died – spiritually unparalyzed and with the full freedom that comes from the hope of salvation.

18. The Blessing of Surrender

When we deny self, we lay everything at the feet of Jesus; not just our families and friends, our homes and our possessions; but our very lives. We disclaim the right of ownership of them all – and their very use and benefit to us.

Most times He chooses to bless us by allowing us to use what we have surrendered while we are here on earth. But sometimes, for no apparent reason, His blessing is demonstrated through His strength.

He offers, instead, Himself, in the place of a lost child, or failing health; the death of a spouse, the agony of divorce, or the pain of a job lost. He becomes the Rock that lifts us above the flood when the momentary foundation of family, or friend, or health or any other thing is not returned for our use.

Christ does not love the ones He blesses with particular temporal foundations any more, or less, than He loves those from whom he does not remove all the thorns of the flesh. And we are not to compare thorns or blossoms on each other, because we are all part of the same plant.

19. The Pink Rabbit

It was hard to miss the man's overt grumbling as he jockeyed for position in the check-out line. He managed to be the fourth person back on a busy Saturday; I fell in right behind him. Not bothering to keep his nastiness to himself, he hurled a continuous string of verbal jabs at the woman who took too long writing her check; the gentleman who needed a price check; and especially the cashier who scanned purchases too slowly for his liking.

A glance into the grumbler's cart revealed a screwdriver and other various tools, batteries and individual frozen meals. An obvious bachelor and for good reason, I concluded – until I saw tucked among the items the most adorable stuffed pink rabbit. It looked velvety and soft, quite unlike the personality of the man in whose cart the tender rabbit lay. I knew there was a story behind that animal.

At that point my curiosity took the reins. "That's a beautiful rabbit you have there," I offered. For the first time the man glanced behind him to see me, appearing glad to have a woman approve his choice.

A single tear started the long trip down his gruff, time-worn face as he gingerly picked up the pink treasure. "It's for my wife," he responded quietly. "She's in the hospital dying. I didn't know what else to get."

Suddenly the Spirit filled me with a sense of care and concern for this snippy shopper. Here was a man with the reality of death at his doorstep and no one to share his agony. I realized there was no time for vague pleasantries; this was a divine appointment.

I told him of the gift of salvation that comes from confession and belief in the Lord Jesus. I shared the hope of heaven where there is no more pain, or suffering or death. I don't remember exactly what I said but it didn't matter. The Holy Spirit was wooing this soul; I was merely the mouthpiece. I was so grateful for the tip-off of a stuffed pink rabbit; and never more thankful for the snail-like pace of a grocery line.

I never saw that man again and I don't know what decision he may have made as a result of our conversation. Life doesn't always present itself in such neatly wrapped packages. I was simply called to be obedient, as all believers are.

20. As One

This is for our fellow believers reading at great cost. We will never forget you.

Father, today we lift up our brothers and sisters around the world. Many of them wake each day to the reality of suffering for the sake of your Name. Daily they face the choice of rejecting you or facing persecution. Because they have put their faith in the salvation of Jesus Christ they are tortured; shot; beheaded; crucified; burned alive. They are shunned; robbed; beaten; kidnapped; raped.

Holy Spirit, give them strength so they do not falter. Grant them the calm assurance of their redemption in the face of temporary torment. May they be bolstered by their trust and confident of their convictions. Bestow upon them the peace that passes understanding that can only be found in you. Bless them with the full measure of your love.

Lord Jesus, thank you for the promise of eternal life to all those who believe that you alone are sufficient; that you paid the price for sin with your death on the cross; that you rose again and are even now preparing a place for us and that you will come again. As long as we have breath, may we proclaim your Name.

We weep with those who weep; we mourn with those who mourn. Father, thank you for the example of stalwart faith our fellow believers demonstrate daily. May we all be united in you; may we be as one.

In Jesus Holy Name,

Amen

21. The Choice

For quite some time I have been suffering from leg weakness, often making it difficult to walk. What is particularly frustrating is that I know the cause; it is a side effect of a medication I take to maintain my kidney transplant. The same drug also makes my feet and ankles swell considerably, meaning it can be hard to stuff my feet into a pair of shoes. Yes, I have worn slippers to church when no other shoes would fit.

My recent trip to the Mayo Clinic finally afforded me the opportunity for which I longed, an opportunity to switch medications. Routine annual tests revealed some issues with the kidney, necessitating a biopsy. That wonder drug I detested was now also contributing to a significant loss of protein in my body. At last, a real medical reason to get rid of the dreaded medication.

Because of the difficulty of my case, my doctor decided to take it to a conference committee of fellow Mayo nephrologists to get a consensus on what regimen I would be prescribed. It was anticipated that I may be placed on a mix of drugs that had never been used in combination, perhaps including infusions. It was intimidating; yet also exhilarating. Perhaps my situation could break ground for future patients. I awaited the follow-up call with great anticipation.

When the ringing phone displayed the Mayo area code, I answered it hastily. It was not secretary or a nurse; it was my doctor calling me directly. My excitement was at a fever pitch. But as I listened to his solemn voice, I heard a completely different assessment, reached after considerable debate among the physicians.

Simply put, I was asked to stay the course: no changes at the moment. I was told that the offending medication had the power to mitigate the side effect of another drug, which contributed to cancer recurrences. Only when my condition worsened would they make a change.

I dejectedly hung up the phone. The long-hoped for liberation for my legs would have to wait. As I fought back tears I realized I had to decide how to deal with this news. I had a choice. In that moment I felt the distinctive presence of the Holy Spirit, who drew me to Him. I had so much for which to be thankful and I knew I had to worship.

I thanked God for my transplant of 22 years and the medications which sustained it; that there were potential options on the horizon when and if they were needed; that I had great medical care and a staff of doctors representing some of the best medical minds in the field on my side; that I was a child of the King, loved and redeemed for eternity. In that brief expression of gratitude, my attitude began to shift. I am not glad that I get no immediate relief from the medication. But I choose to focus on the blessings. That in no way makes me exceptional. It makes me obedient, which is what all believers are called to be.

22. Because

There was no two ways about it; the kids were brats. They had such a bad reputation that by now no one would give the beleaguered parents an evening off, much less a whole weekend. People said they were crazy when they decided to become licensed foster parents. After all, their own children had long since grown and were out of the house. This was the time to enjoy their golden years; at least that's what their friends said.

But they fostered anyway. And when the call came to accept two precious little girls so the sisters would not have to be split up, they couldn't resist. They were just getting settled into a semblance of a routine when they got the call that their older sister was now out of residential treatment. Wouldn't it be grand if they gave the blessing of family to this delightful, if not slightly misguided teen? What's one more, they reasoned? And so it began.

These two incredible people were determined to keep their commitment in spite of the daily challenges. They showered those three sisters with love, attention and a healthy dose of discipline. But they finally needed a break – a weekend away to rest and rejuvenate. By then word had gotten around to all the approved respite providers. Interestingly, not one was available any time for the foreseeable future.

I guess I could have volunteered. I had quit my position as supervisor of the private foster care agency, through whom these parents were licensed, in anticipation of an upcoming move. My husband was already working in the new location. I could sense the desperation in the caseworker's voice. She had promised these dedicated foster parents their weekend and there was literally no one else. I grudgingly consented.

"What a sacrifice I am making," I told myself. I could be home relaxing and now I have to spend the entire weekend with these mischief-makers. I didn't enjoy one moment of the first night, and neither did they. It wasn't until the next afternoon that I allowed the Holy Spirit's voice to penetrate. The conviction hit hard. I could finish muddling through the weekend feeling sorry for myself. Or I could dedicate this time to the Lord and do it for His glory.

I had promised the time to this family; why not make a gift of it? In that moment I decided to complete my task as an offering to God. I decided to do it out of love: for Him who deserves our best; for the parents who needed a short break; and for the girls, who did not ask for the circumstances in their family which were the genesis of their issues.

The girls did not instantly become candidates for sainthood. But we survived the weekend together and I actually enjoyed my time. The needed change had occurred in me. It happened when the reason I was doing it was altered. The "because" made all the difference.

23. Persistent

Whether we believe the tenets of the Bible cannot be based on the impulses of the world. God help us if we possess a faith so flimsy that it can be shouted down in the public square; that we can be intimidated either by black flags or splashes of color; that we are threatened out of holding fast to the assurance of our salvation.

We were never promised a primrose path. Indeed, we who cling to Christian convictions are guaranteed opposition. In the midst of first century persecution, the Apostle Peter admonishes believers not to be surprised at fiery trials. "But rejoice inasmuch as you participate in the sufferings of Christ, so that you may be overjoyed when his glory is revealed. If you are insulted because of the name of Christ, you are blessed, for the Spirit of glory and of God rests on you." 1 Peter 4:13-14 (NIV).

Notice that Peter did not say trials were optional. Nor did he instruct us to invite hardship – merely that it is inevitable if we are living out our lives as followers of Christ. For some this means the ultimate challenge of cleaving to the doctrine of truth or facing execution. For others, it may mean loss of home, family, job, status, respect or any number of other consequences. But our beliefs are not based on whether this world joins, or even accepts, our ranks. Our trust is in the Ancient of Days, the Alpha and Omega, the King of Kings.

We believe in God the Father, Jesus the Son and the Holy Spirit as three in One. We believe that He sent Jesus to earth to pay the price for our sins in His substitutionary death on the cross; that He was resurrected; that He has gone to heaven and will return; that all who profess His Name and follow Him will one day be in heaven forever with Him.

May we hold fast to what we believe; May we remain united in our stand.

24. Two Lines

Following the brief graveside ceremony the veteran's representative solemnly approached Dad. He gently explained that one side of Mom's marker would display her name and the dates of birth and death, as well as Dad's branch of service and rank. If desired, the second side would have a tribute to her. It was limited to two lines of fifteen characters each, and included spaces and punctuation.

In the cold winter air I gazed at the rolling hills of white markers, evenly spaced, and the grounds meticulously kept. All the relatives of the deceased buried in the hallowed grounds of this veteran's cemetery were given the same opportunity: sum up the life of a loved one in two short lines. I wondered how many strolled through the graveyard, noticing the inscriptions.

"We should say something about her being a loving wife and mother," one of us said. "She loved her grandchildren so much," another contributed. We all had ideas and shared them with Dad, although the decision rested solely with him. Leave it to Dad. He wanted even her last symbol to let others know of her faith, hopefully prompting readers to contemplate their own eternal fates.

He wanted the marker to read "At home with the Lord". And so she is.

25. Hope

"And I heard a loud voice from heaven saying, 'Behold, the tabernacle of God is with men, and He will dwell with them, and they shall be His people, and God Himself will be with them and be their God. And God will wipe away every tear from their eyes; there shall be no more death, nor sorrow, nor crying; and there shall be no more pain, for the former things have passed away.'" Revelation 21:3-4.

I know that when my life on earth is ended I will be with God in heaven. That is the source of my ultimate hope. But hope on a daily basis in the midst of struggle is much more difficult to maintain. It fades; it must be fed and nurtured.

We must allow others to see the confidence that lives in us. 1 Peter 3:15 instructs believers: "But sanctify the Lord God in your hearts, and always be ready to give a defense to everyone who asks you a reason for the hope that is in you, with meekness and fear." When the people around us see the hope we carry with us through crises, we then have the opportunity to share the Source of that hope.

"Whoever is thirsty, let him come; and whoever wishes, let him take the free gift of the water of life." May all who read, come to share this eternal hope.

26. Jay

At the time, I knew virtually nothing about professional baseball and had no desire to learn. But when Jay heard I was dating a great guy who loved the sport and the Kansas City team in particular, he went right to work. He not only insisted that I had to memorize the entire starting line-up of the Kansas City Royals, he tested me until I got it right. He assured me it would impress my future husband – and he was right. His bright smile came with a "You're welcome," when I showed him my engagement ring. Of course Mike had to meet the man who "put me over the top" and sealed the deal for our marriage.

But Jay was so much more than baseball statistics and love of the game. He and his wife, Sharon, loved the Lord and it showed in the way they raised their daughters and their faithfulness in service. They prayed fervently for me in the midst of my early struggles with lupus and meningitis. They made me feel loved and treasured at a time I felt ugly and vulnerable.

When I became a young church youth leader, they saw past my blunders and encouraged me. They opened their home to the rag-tag group of teens and their novice leader, shepherding both with wisdom and understanding.

I don't know why Jay had to suffer from Parkinson's disease. I don't know why he didn't get the miracle of healing on this side of heaven. What I do know is that I will see him again because we share a faith in the saving grace of our Lord Jesus Christ.

Holy Spirit, grant his family comfort in the midst of loss; peace through the tears and an overwhelming sense of your presence. Amen.

27. Grasping Life

"Her name is Lisa," the young mother barked at the nurse. Rachel yanked the baby carrier up from the floor and stormed from the waiting room, back to see the doctor. Rachel fell into a chair and waited mechanically for the nurse to take Lisa's vital signs. This was a teenager who had long ago lost everything - her parents, her siblings, her home - but most of all, her innocence.

Rachel hadn't planned on getting pregnant. In her world being agreeable to the demands of a guy meant receiving attention and caring; it was as simple as that. So what if the affection wasn't real? It was better than the loneliness of being ignored, and she had had plenty of that to last a lifetime. She had been shuffled from one foster home to another and was now in a group home.

Lisa was sick again, which meant Rachel had to leave school. She didn't mind another day away from a strange junior high where the other students seemed only to gawk and walk away from her. But she could think of a thousand other ways to spend it besides sitting in a cold doctor's office with a crying baby whose whining had kept her up most of the night.

Rachel got easily frustrated with Lisa. Not only did she seem a constant disruption, she cramped any plan Rachel had, such that it was. What was she going to do with her life? How would she support Lisa? Who would help her? Yet Rachel never once seriously considered placing Lisa for adoption.

Rachel might not know how her life was going to go, but in her eyes, she suddenly had a real-life human being who would love her unconditionally, be there for her, look up to her and play with her. That's a lot to expect of a three-month-old baby. But Rachel, still somewhere between a woman and a girl, never got to experience a real childhood. She never remembered being fed without an adult griping about the effort. She never even had a doll.

And so, Rachel carries with her a distorted view of what life is meant to be, and of how people were meant to interact with each other. She growls with regularity and is understandably suspicious of any kindness. Yet if it takes a thousand kind gestures, mixed with gentle expectations and the demonstration of another way of life, I am convinced that it is worth the effort. There is hope for Rachel, which means there is hope for Lisa. Let's never stop loving the Rachels among us, even while they are grasping at what life is supposed to be.

28. Heart Cry

Today as I read my Bible and prayed, my heart began to grieve for fellow Christians currently under attack. It is happening in a city written about in the Bible.

Over 2,700 years ago a prophet named Jonah was called to the Assyrian capital of Nineveh to proclaim the Word of the Lord. A direct warning was given to all who refused to acknowledge and obey Him. Nineveh is now known as Mosul, Iraq. The name has changed but the enduring struggle for souls in that land has been reignited.

The ancient tomb of Jonah has been destroyed, a mere symbol of what invaders planned to do to all believers there who refuse to renounce Christ. They were to convert, flee or be killed. It was that straightforward.

Quite simply, the Christians in Mosul are deciding how much their faith means to them: the loss of freedom, possessions and even their very lives are on the line. If the men plotting evil have their way, that land once again will have people living there whose aim is to silence all praise to the God of heaven. Left unchecked, their ultimate goal is to mute the voices of Christians everywhere.

We are called to rejoice with those who rejoice, mourn with those who mourn and hurt with those who hurt. This day as my brothers and sisters in the Lord face persecution because of their beliefs, my heart is broken for them.

Lyrics to an old song written by the Gaithers (This Is the Time I Must Sing; 1975) include a phrase that seems appropriate in light of this battle. "If the rocks would cry out, should His praises die out, then the stones must keep silent. As long as I've breath for the singing, His praise will keep ringing and I will keep singing my song."

Terrorists may be able to temporarily squelch the sound of godly praise from Mosul; but they will never be able to quiet the multitudes of believers around the world whose devotion to the truth of the Gospel is strong and unwavering. May we be ever unified in our heart cry of praise to the Savior and in unceasing intercession for those in our faith family who are under attack.

29. The Purse

It wasn't hard to sort her clothes. It was done in a hurry so we could get Dad moved from assisted living to our house. The precious mementos Dad selected and sent her while serving in Germany were put aside for the moment. There is plenty of time for all of us to go through them together. Mounds of medicine were next, followed by mountains of paperwork.

The stack of things to organize kept shrinking. Finally there was almost nothing left in the corner but one black object. It certainly didn't look intimidating, as it was simply made of sturdy black plastic with two short straps to fit over her wrist.

I made myself approach it. I even picked it up at one point, telling myself it was high time to peek into all the zippered compartments and hidden sections. I knew I would find her identification card, which had replaced the driver's license when she could no longer navigate the van on her own. There would be credit cards, receipts, family pictures and a tiny black comb. But there may also still be scribbled notes from a hand that had become unable to write coherently; shopping lists of groceries never purchased; and coupons from a wish list.

It seems like such a silly thing, to be unable to examine a now-innocuous item. But grief is personal and makes no sense; it has no distinguishable rhythm. If I could, I would sit on my bed and hold it and cry a thousand tears. But Dad is in the other room, dealing with his loss through the prism of memory loss – and likely to appear in the doorway any time to show me a picture he has shown me only moments before and will show me again repeatedly throughout the day.

So I force back the tears; they will have to wait another day. Until then, Mom's purse will sit in the corner collecting dust.

30. Getting Home

Sure enough; when the rain stopped in time for everyone to gather at the park, I started hearing it. "Isn't God so good to answer our prayers?" one woman gushed. "He's blessing us again," another replied. Don't get me wrong. I believe that the Lord does sometimes bless His children with sunshine. Other times He chooses to bless farmers with rain.

My fear is that simplistic views of sunny-day picnics can cloud what we believe about God's intervention - or lack thereof – in the bigger realms of our lives. What if we have learned that God's goodness means the tumor is certainly benign; that Dad will never get Alzheimer's; and that travelers will always arrive at their destinations? What if we begin to equate God's goodness with His bestowal of materialistic miracles?

The truth is that people do die. Sometimes we may get glimpses of glory as beloved saints pass from this life into eternity. But that is the exception. Often there is prolonged illness, suffering and pain. Test results make us cry. We wipe away tears when loved ones no longer remember our names. We sob when we receive word of a horrific wreck that kills members of our communities.

Recently I returned from the Mayo Clinic, after having to be biopsied yet again for recurrent cancer. I nodded as well-meaning individuals praised God for a good report. Indeed, praise was warranted. Yet on behalf of the many believers whose reports indicated otherwise, I wanted to shout, "But if the cancer had returned, God's still good!" God's character does not change based on how I perceive His gift-giving.

Perhaps in our humanness, we sometimes lose sight of the fact that we Christians have to get home somehow. We are not all destined to fall asleep one night and wake up in heaven. There may be suffering and pain; surgeries and vigils; tears and agony. But even these momentary sorrows cannot compare to the joys we will share when we are finally and forever in the presence of our Redeemer. May His Name be praised, regardless of our circumstance.

www.ingramcontent.com/pod-product-compliance
Lightning Source LLC
Chambersburg PA
CBHW071836020426
42331CB00007B/1741